Acres and Pains

Acres and Pains

By S. J. Perelman
WITH DRAWINGS BY HANK BLAUSTEIN

Lyons & Burford, Publishers

Printed in the United States of America
Design by Cindy LaBreacht

10 9 8 7 6 5 4 3 2 1

Perelman, S. J. (Sidney Joseph), 1904–
    Acres and pains / by S. J. Perelman; with drawings by H. Blaustein.
    p.   cm.
    Originally published: New York : Reynals & Hitchcock, 1947.
    ISBN: 1-55821-359-7
    1. Country life—Pennsylvania—Humor.   2. Country life—
Pennsylvania—Anecdotes.   I. Title.
PN6231.C65P47   1995
818'.5203—dc20
[B]   94-24655
                                               CIP

Thanks are due to The Saturday Evening Post *and* The Country Book *for permission to reprint that material which has appeared in their pages.*

To Ruth and Gus

ONE

If you can spare the time to drive sixty miles into the backwoods of eastern Pennsylvania, crouch down in a bed of poison ivy, and peer through the sumacs, you will be rewarded by an interesting sight. What you will see is a middle-aged city dweller, as lean and bronzed as a shad's belly (I keep a shad's belly hanging up in the barn for purposes of comparison), gnawing his

fingernails and wondering how to abandon a farm. Outside of burning down the buildings, I have tried every known method to dispose of it. I have raffled it off, let the taxes lapse, staked it on the turn of a card, and had it condemned by the board of health. I have cut it up into building lots which proved unsalable, turned it over to picnic parties who promptly turned it back. I have sidled up to strangers and whispered hoarsely, "Psst, brother, want to buy a hot farm?" only to have them call a policeman. One rainy day, in desperation, I even tried desertion. Lowering a dory, I shouted, "Stern all for your lives!" and began sculling away rapidly. Unfortunately, I had forgotten to remove the flowers that grew in the boat, and nightfall found me still on the lawn with a backache and a fearful head cold.

I began my career as a country squire with nothing but a high heart, a flask of citronella, and a fork for toasting marshmallows in case supplies ran low. In a scant fifteen years I have acquired a superb library of mortgages, mostly first editions, and the finest case of sacroiliac known to science. In that period I made several important discoveries. The first was that there are no chiggers in an air-cooled movie and that a corner delicatessen at dusk is more exciting than any rainbow. On a fine night, no matter how fragrant the scent of the nicotiana, I can smell the sharp pungency of a hot corned-beef sandwich all the way from New York. I also learned that to lock horns with Nature, the only equipment you really need is the constitution of Paul Bunyan and the basic training of a commando. Most of the handbooks on country living are written by flabby men at the Waldorf-Astoria, who lie in bed and dictate them to secretaries. The greatest naturalist I know lives in a penthouse overlooking Central Park. He hasn't raised his window shades in twenty years.

Actually I never would have found myself in the middle of eighty-three unimproved acres had I been a bit less courteous. One day back in 1932, I was riding a crosstown trolley in Manhattan when I noticed a little old lady swaying before me, arms laden with bundles. Though almost thirty, she was very well preserved; her hair was ash-blonde, her carmine lips wore a mocking pout, and there was such helpless innocence in her eyes that I sprang to her rescue. Dislodging the passenger next to me, I offered her the seat and we fell into conversation. It soon developed that we had both been reared in the country and shared a mutual love for wildflowers and jam. At the next stop, I persuaded her to accompany me to a wildflower-and-jam store where we could continue our chat. It was only after our fifth glass of jam that my new friend confided her desperate plight. Her aged parents were about to be evicted from their farm unless she could raise five hundred dollars immediately. Through sheer coincidence, I happened to have drawn that amount from the bank to buy my wife a fur coat. Knowing that she would have done likewise, I pressed it on the fair stranger and signed some sort of document, the exact nature of which escaped me. After a final round of jam, she presented me with her card and left, vowing eternal gratitude. On examining it, I noticed a curious inscription in fine print. It read, "Licensed Real-Estate Agent."

I still have the card in my upper bureau drawer. Right next to it, in a holster, is a Smith & Wesson .38 I'm holding in escrow for the lady the next time we meet. And we will—don't you worry. I've got plenty of patience. That's one thing you develop in the country.

TWO

Outside of a spring lamb trotting into the slaughterhouse, there is nothing in the animal kingdom as innocent and foredoomed as the new purchaser of a country place. The moment he scratches his signature on the deed, it is open season and no limit to the bag. At once, Nature starts cutting him down to size. Wells that bubbled over for two hundred years mysteriously go dry, stone walls develop huge fissures, and chimneys sag out of plumb. Majestic elms which have withstood the full fury of the hurricane and the Dutch blight begin shedding their leaves; oaks dating from the reign of Charles II fade like cheap calico. Meanwhile, the former owner is busy removing a few personal effects. He rolls up the lawn preparatory to loading it on flatcars, floats the larger trees downstream, and carts off the corncrib, woodshed and toolhouse. When I first viewed my own property, my dewy naïveté was incredible—even Dewey Naïveté, the agent who showed me around, had to suppress a smile. What sealed the choice was a decrepit henhouse occupied by a flock of

white Wyandottes. According to my estimate, it needed only a vigorous dusting and a small can of enamel to transform it into a snug guest cottage. Shading my eyes, I could see the magnificent wisteria, heavy with blooms, creeping up a lattice any amateur could construct with ten cents' worth of nails. As soon as I took possession, though, I discovered that it must have been on casters, for all that greeted me was a yawning pit trimmed with guano and eggshells.

This baptism, however, was merely a prelude to the keelhauling the natives had in store. Like any greenhorn from the city, I used to choke up freely at the sight of the man with the hoe. Every bumpkin I encountered reminded me of Daniel Webster; his dreariest platitude had the dignity and sweep of Walt Whitman's verse. Selecting one noble old patriarch, who I was sure had served with John Brown at Harpers Ferry, I commissioned him to paint the barn. Several days later, he notified me that forty-seven gallons were exhausted. "No use skimpin'," he warned. "A hickory stump, a widow woman and a barn has to be protected from the weather." I was chuckling over this bit of folk wisdom without quite understanding it when I detected a slight bulge under his coat similar to that caused by a five-gallon drum. He intercepted my glance and informed me fluently that he usually picked a few cranberries during his lunch hour. Apparently he lunched on Cape Cod, five hundred miles to the north, but since he never took more than half an hour, I overlooked it and ordered more paint. A week afterward, his barn burst forth in a shade of red identical with mine.

"Looks like yours, don't it?" He grinned. "Durned if I can tell 'em apart." I knew what he meant.

I have been taken to the cleaners since by some notable brigands, but the most brazen of the lot was the kinsman of Jesse James who repaired our road. Edward Mittendorf and his merry men spent a fortnight lounging about in well-cut slacks, pitching quoits and reading Kierkegaard. Occasionally one of the more enterprising workmen would saunter over and deposit a pinch of gravel daintily in the ruts. Whenever my wife passed by, the crew appraised her charms, whistling and clucking spiritedly. I entered a mild demurrer and received the following instructions: "You tell 'em, corset; you've been around the ladies." The day of settlement dawned on schedule, and with

Mittendorf watching me beadily, I began to examine his bill. It was a closely typewritten document resembling the annual report of the Federal Reserve. Among other items he listed depreciation on shovels, lemonades for the men, and some bridgework his niece had ordered.

"Who's Ed Mittendorf?" I inquired, indicating a salary in excess of Cary Grant's.

"My cousin—the little fat feller," he explained.

"Is he the same as Eddie Mittendorf?" I asked.

"No, that's my dad," he returned smoothly, "and Ned Mittendorf there, he's my uncle. I'm Edward—got that straight?"

"I should," I snapped. "Your name's down here twice."

"It is?" he gasped. "Well, I swan."

I swanned also on reading the total, but I paid through the nose, a locale which was rapidly taking on the aspect of a teller's window. If you ever drive up the lane, be careful. Those diamonds raise hell with your treads.

THREE

I wouldn't live in the city if you paid me a million dollars a year—well, let's say forty-two dollars a year. How people can exist side by side with utter disregard for each other, never prying into anybody's business, is beyond me. In the country, folks are more matey; there is always an extra stiletto for the newcomer and a friendly hand ready to tighten around his throat. The

moving men have hardly kicked the rungs out of your
Chippendale chairs before neighbors spring up like
mushrooms, eager to point out any flaws you may
have missed in your place and gloat over your
predicament. My wife and I were still knee-deep in
a puddle outside our front door, exchanging shrill
taunts and questioning each other's legitimacy, when
our first visitor drove up. Shearing off an irreplace-
able dogwood, he pulled into a flower bed and got
out. From the expression of mingled condescension,
malice and envy, I knew at once he must be another
city man turned farmer. As his gaze traveled slowly
over the *estancia*, he took on the look of one who has
just bitten into an unripe persimmon.

"Finally unloaded it, did they?" he remarked
with a ghoulish smirk.

"What do you mean?" I asked, my hackles rising to attention.

"The old pesthouse," he said intimately. "So
they found a simp to take it off their hands."

"Oh, I don't know," I said with what started out
as dignity but wound up as a girlish toss of the head.
He examined my clothes intently. "You the hired man?"
he asked at length.

"No, the simp," I snarled. There was a brief interval during which I could hear his watch ticking.

"No hard feelings, brother," he said eventually. "Nice little spot you've got here. My name's Grundy." He held out his hand.

"Mine's Frankenstein," I said, ignoring it, "and this is the Monster," I added, indicating my wife.

"Glad to know you, Mrs. Monster," he acknowledged. "I see you're having trouble with your foundation."

"I *beg* your pardon," she snapped with considerable hauteur, furtively smoothing her hips.

"I mean, of course, the house," Grundy corrected himself. "I saw your husband creeping around under the porch a while ago."

"Oh, he was just rooting for truffles," she said sweetly. As she stalked off, Grundy smacked his lips. "Some package," he commented. "Where'd a little shrimp like you ever meet her?"

"Listen here, my friend," I began, taking a step toward him.

"Yes," he said thoughtfully, "you've got plenty of things to worry about. You'll never be able to drink the water—it's tainted. And that woodwork of yours is alive with termites. What did you give for this root cellar?"

"Nothing," I lied. "We took it for a bad debt."

"Well, you were stung," said Grundy. "Come here." He approached one of the windows, and whipping out a jackknife, slashed at the casings. Several panes of glass shivered into fragments on the ground. "Putty's rotten," he said triumphantly. "It's the talk of the countryside. And that's not all. See that stream down there? Every spring it rises to the second story. You'll be doubled up with rheumatism, if the mosquitoes don't get you first. You know, I never saw the shack by daylight before; no wonder they say it's haunted. Now, you take my place—"

We took his place. It had thirty-five rooms and ten baths—snug but adequate for his needs. The attic was hand-hewn out of solid cherry, with burled walnut floors. For odd jobs he employed a lineal descendant of Cellini; whom he paid off in green trading stamps; the latter had just remodeled the barn into a game room and servants' quarters at a total cost of $2.76. The soil was none too fertile, he admitted—it took a week for tomatoes to bear and his dahlias were only a foot across. But there were so many trout in his creek that you could walk across without wetting your feet.

"Tell you what I'd do if I were you," he con-
cluded. "I'd pitch a tent outside and use the dwelling
for a cow stable. Only watch out where you camp; the
grass is full of black widows." He left, whistling the
"Dead March" from *Saul,* and I entered the house to
find my wife in tears. She cried for six days and on the
seventh created apple butter. It was good, but not like
the woman's next door.

FOUR

Every now and then on a breathless August evening, I like to draw up my easy chair before a glowing fire, puff on a calabash and stare thoughtfully into the flames. The heat is unendurable and the calabash makes me nauseated, but like a bachelor remembering his summer sweethearts, it helps me recall the architects who have almost remodeled my quaint old stone farmhouse. For the money I have spent on blueprints alone, I could have razed the house, erected a replica of the Taj Mahal, and retired to Sun Valley. If I ever adopt a coat of arms, it will show a ravenous draftsman sighting through a transit, over a shield marked "Soft Pickings."

The most recent architect I engaged was as typical as any. He came highly recommended by my attorney, Newmown Hay, of Ashen, Livid and Hay, a profound student of the dollar. From Hay's account, he had just converted a decrepit feed mill into a lordly mansion complete with ballroom and interior squash courts for a little more than $200. The cost would have been half, the architect explained, if Hay had not insisted on marble stairs. The man seemed to have a shrewd eye for values and I crisply outlined my needs—five rooms, three baths, a sun porch, a rumpus room and a tennis court. He made a hasty calculation on the back of my collar and informed me it would cost $1500. I am not one to haggle over pennies and I signed a contract forthwith. He collected fifty clams as a token of good faith—my good faith—and arranged to inspect the premises shortly.

His arrival coincided unhappily with that of an

actor named Cagney, who had dropped in to borrow a cup of film and was exclaiming over my freesias—people came from as far as ten feet around to exclaim over my freesias. The architect kept staring suspiciously at him while I was posing my problem. "I've seen that man somewhere before," he said accusingly.

"Yes, yes," I murmured. "Now if we extend this wing to here—" Suddenly I realized I had lost my audience; he had sneaked up the slope and was peering narrowly at Cagney from behind a syringa bush.

"Listen," he whispered excitedly, clutching my arm. "I can't place this bird, but he's wanted by the police! I got a hunch I saw his picture in a post office—I never forget a face." All at once his jaw dropped and he uttered a squeal. "It's Cagney!" he shrilled. "James Cagney!" Before I could intercede, he had pinned his quarry to the fence, and was re-enacting his favorite scenes in the latter's movies. I fought my way in between them, vainly attempting to restore the architect to his senses.

"I want the master bedroom facing north!" I shouted desperately. "Then we can put the kitchen in the cellar—I mean, the cellar in the attic!" The architect tried to shake me off, but I clung, and we rocked about the lawn like three dancing bears. Finally I managed to loosen his grip, and he made a cursory, grumbling survey of the house.

"It's a mess," he said. "but maybe I can save it." When I suggested he look inside, he grew pale with fury. "Are you trying to teach me my own business?" he snapped. In leaving, he asked Cagney for a small loan, implying that I would probably chisel him out of his fee. I eventually persuaded him to accept a check for a hundred on account, though it was plain he would have preferred cash.

The following Monday, at three o'clock in the morning, he phoned me with a frantic appeal for another hundred; his wife was just undergoing a serious operation. In the background I could hear the characteristic tumult of a hospital amphitheater—the strains of a juke box, the tinkle of ice, and a male quartet singing "Hold That Tiger." The patient subsequently had two relapses, each of which cost me an additional sawbuck. By the time I got the preliminary sketches, Sir Christopher Wren had put the bite on me for four hundred dollars. The first contractor I consulted estimated the job at $21,942. The second was unable to read the plans. The third, who took the job, had a nervous breakdown a week later.

Six months afterward I met the architect on Fifth Avenue with a friend. He cut me dead, and as I passed him I heard him say, "See that little sneak? If I had the money he owes me, I'd be in clover."

FIVE

The events of last Saturday afternoon may be summarized briefly as follows: At 2:30 I was dozing on the porch of my rustic retreat, in tune with the infinite and my fellow man. Above my head, instead of the usual saw biting through a log labeled "Z-z-z," was an acetylene torch cutting a steel girder; there is no room on the up-to-date farm for antiquated methods. At 2:35, roused from my reverie by my wife's broom, I was toiling up a ninety-degree incline with two king-sized pails of garbage. At 2:37, with a report like a pistol crack, several vertebrae went off duty, and by three o'clock I was back on my porch, reeking of liniment and watching my wife toil up the incline with the pails. Painful as it was to turn my head, I gamely spurred her on, and were it not for my constant inspiration and advice, she might never have completed her mission.

Every time I step off that porch, something disastrous happens. The worst mistake the owner of a country place can make is choosing a role too ambitious for his talents. A recent neighbor of mine, for instance, found a lawn mower left by the previous tenant. He immediately began pushing it around in the hot sun, unaware that grass dies back anyhow after a sharp frost. Today that man is a hopeless wreck in a sanitarium, shattered in mind and body. When I first settled down on a heap of shale in the Delaware Valley, I too had a romantic picture of myself. For about a month I was a spare, sinewy frontiersman in fringed buckskin, with crinkly little lines about the eyes and a slow laconic drawl. One look told you that my ringing ax and long Kentucky rifle would tame the forest in jigtime. In fact, as I stepped off the train, I overheard a native remark admiringly, "His ringing ax and long Kentucky rifle should tame the forest in jigtime."

After I almost blew off a toe cleaning an air rifle, though, I decided I was more the honest rural type. I started wearing patched blue jeans, mopped my forehead with a red banana (I found out later it should have been a red bandanna), and crumbled bits of earth between my fingers to see whether it was friable enough. Friable enough for what I wasn't quite sure, but I kept at it until my wife screamed like a banshee if I so much as picked up a clod. I never entered our kitchen like a normal individual; I always stamped in roaring, "Well, mother, got plenty of vittles for the menfolk? Thrashin' sure makes a man hongry!" The upshot was that the hired girl started leaving a couple of sandwiches behind the barn. I even went so far as to buy a good secondhand tractor. It was dirt cheap, as the engine had disappeared; nevertheless, I got some really effective snapshots of myself against the horizon. At sundown, when the day's loafing was done, I generally repaired to the village store with a quid of cut plug in my cheek, and spent the evening sullenly spitting on my bluchers and cursing the Administration. Sometimes I did a little whittling, but just because a few measly shavings fell into the cracker barrel, the postmaster made a neurotic, half-hysterical scene and I took my custom elsewhere.

It was nearly two years before I discovered my true identity. One day, while stretched out on the porch, I realized I needed only a mint julep to become a real dyed-in-the-wool, Seagram's V.V.O. Southern planter. I promptly barked a command, which was ignored. Instead, my wife appeared and confronted me, arms akimbo. "Who do you think you are, you lug?" she demanded. "A Southern planter?" I knew at once my instinct was right and, dismissing her with a cut of my riding crop, set to work assembling the necessary gear. I sent to New York for a broad-brimmed hat and string tie, and at enormous expense trained the local idiot to fan me with a palmetto leaf. Procuring a no-account hound-dog was more difficult; every kennel I wrote to stocked thoroughbreds, so I was finally forced to buy one and starve it into submission. It has taken a lack of energy and a shiftlessness few men are capable of, but after eight years you can't tell me from the genuine article—at least, that's what the hookworms say. Up to last Saturday I never once budged off that porch. Well, I've only myself to blame. I guess I'm my own worst enemy.

SIX

There is nothing like a farm, a mountain lodge or a seashore bungalow to bring out the latent mechanic in a man. Once the deed is filed and he stands alone at last with his utilities, he is Cortez on a peak in Darien. Of course, if your name is Cortez and you live on a peak in Darien, Connecticut, your problem is simple. You call in a plumber from Danbury and forget about it. I

couldn't; when I returned to the soil, I had a ten-cent screwdriver and the mechanical skill of a turtle. Today, thanks to unremitting study, I can change a fuse so deftly that it plunges the entire county into darkness. The neighbors call me "the boy Steinmetz" and things like that (the other things are shorter). The power company has offered me as high as fifteen thousand dollars a year to stay out of my own cellar.

The other night, for example, I had invited some guests to dinner at Hysteria Hall and we were grouped around the groaning board (the board was groaning because one end was supported by a chair until I could replace the missing leg). Halfway through the meal, a strident clanking began under our very feet, as though somebody were striking the furnace with a length of chain. I raised my voice to drown it out, but I could see my audience was wool-gathering. At first I suspected my wife, who will resort to the most shameless devices to spoil an anecdote. Then I realized she was flinching in concert with the company. The noise redoubled. "Sounds like chains, doesn't it?" I stammered desperately. "You know, this house was a station on the Underground Railway, and there's an old legend—"

I was interrupted by a bubbling effect, as of water seeping through a dining-room floor, and looked down to find an inch or two of moisture lapping at my oxfords. Before I could explain that we had chosen a low, marshy situation to remind us of the English lake country, my wife rose through a jet of live steam like the devil in Faust and placed a monkey wrench beside my plate. I pretended it was part of the meal, a pantomime which threw my guests into gales of silence, and slunk off into the cellar.

As one who flunked trigonometry four times, it took me only a moment to detect the source of the trouble. That little square business on the electric pump—I forget just what they call it—had worked off. This in turn disengaged the stopcock or the bushing (it was a bit too dark to tell which) in such a way that the hot water was feeding into the coal bin instead of the storage tank, or flange. The whole thing was clearly the work of a master criminal, perhaps Professor Moriarty himself, who had further anticipated my movements and laid a carpet sweeper athwart the stairs. I sidestepped neatly, but my head encountered a low rafter and I sustained a bruise roughly the size of a robin's egg; I speak of this with certainty as there chanced to be a robin's egg lying on a nearby shelf. Luckily, I am as tough as nails, and picking myself up at the bottom of the steps, I set to work. By exerting a slight leverage, I succeeded in prying off the gasket, or outer jacket of the pump, exactly as you would a baked potato. (I describe this simply so that even the layman can understand.) This gave me room to poke around the innards with a sharp stick. I cleaned the pump thoroughly, laid all the different wheels and cams on a board where the plumber could find them and, as a final precaution, opened the windows to allow the water to drain off down the slope.

On the way upstairs, I found my passage blocked by a jug of peach brandy, and after some difficulty managed to squeeze past it. Either it was stuffy in the basement or I had given too freely of my strength, for when I rejoined the party, I felt dizzy. My wife said later it wasn't so much the bric-a-brac I smashed as the language I used. It cost me a quart of Bellodgia and a star sapphire to square the rap, to say nothing of a new electric pump. However, the old one was nearly played out. Anybody could have seen it with half an eye—and I had that, Jack.

SEVEN

Webster's Collegiate Dictionary, which has a crew haircut, a class pipe and a yellow oilskin slicker, describes a farm as "a piece of land leased for cultivation, hence any tract devoted to agricultural purposes." I prefer my own definition. A farm is an irregular patch of nettles bounded by short-term notes, containing a fool and his wife who didn't know enough to stay in

41

the city. In addition, it usually contains a curious piece of statuary that comes to life at mealtimes and answers to the name of Lafe. I have had seven handy men named Lafe since I went back to the soil. One of them was really two twelve-year-old boys who stood on each other's shoulders and shirked as a team. I never could determine their names, as I only speak three languages, but I made out the check to Lafe and it managed to get cashed.

I found the master, or original Lafe, in the weeds near the house one morning after we moved in. His mouth was open and a wren had built a nest in it. I started to train a vine over him, thinking he was part of the lattice, when he yawned suddenly. His first words were characteristic. "She's a white elephant," he said with gloomy relish. "She'll bankrupt you. You'll rue the day—" I had already heard the same aria sung by my bride and was in no mood for an encore. Thrusting a hatchet into his nerveless fingers, I indicated I needed firewood more than a forecast. An hour later I heard a sickening crash and ran out to find our most stately maple lying across the henhouse.

"No sense goin' all the way to the wood lot," commented Lafe. "She'd have blown over in the next storm anyway."

His successor was a gnarled old salt on the order of Popeye, with a face the color of teak and a gold earring. He had followed the sea from boyhood, having spent thirty-five years cleaning fish in Camden, New Jersey. His rolling walk quickly became more pronounced when he discovered the key to my liquor closet. At first he confined himself fastidiously to the rarer champagnes, but in time he let down the bars and would drink Scotch if forced to the wall. One morning, rummaging through the cellar, I came across him reclining face down in a puddle of Benedictine.

"Tastes just like candy, don't it?" he cackled. "Say, mate, I was looking over your wife yesterday. Cute little dish, ain't she?" I paid him off in Spanish doubloons and he departed, gaily humming a chantey. With him went a pair of my best cuff links and a dozen spoons.

He was followed by a drooping, melancholy individual who felt it was useless to plant vegetables or flowers, as the cutworm and the aphid were bound to get them eventually. According to advices he had received, the Japanese beetle was due to take over a week from Tuesday and it was flying in the face of

The Lafes

Providence to resist. Most of this worthy's day was spent discussing his diseases, by far the most complex assortment ever suffered by mortal man. He was taking radio treatments for diabetes from a hex doctor in Allentown, the blood clot on his brain was the despair of the medical world, and his legs were slowly turning to stone from overexertion in his youth. Despite a touch of arthritis and a few adhesions, however, he ate like a wolf and slept fourteen hours a night. He was still sleepy the second day when I drove him to the junction to catch the evening train. I asked him about his future plans. He figured he might go out to the Mayo Clinic for a while. He hadn't wanted to alarm me, but his milt was enlarged three times its normal size.

My present Lafe is a man of varied talents. He has been successively a comic artist, a scenario writer and a playwright. In appearance he suggests the Apollo Belvedere, though his brain has the same specific gravity as that of Blaise Pascal. To watch him swing a scythe or clean a cistern is an experience to curl your hair. Under his guidance the farm has become a show place, producing blights and fungi unknown to botany. For my part, he's got a lifetime

EIGHT

As though everyone hasn't trouble enough, a little group of research workers—played by Paul Muni—at the Rockefeller Foundation—played by Morris Carnovsky—has recently been inducing nervous breakdowns in dogs. The boys have been feeding Fido mock hamburger, strafing him with squadrons of heavy-duty fleas, and setting him loose on lifelike burgers made of cardboard. A week of this treatment turns the average dog into a hopeless neurotic, and Dame Rumor—played by Dame May Whitty—has it that they mean to extend the experiments to humans. If so, I can save them considerable time and money with a modest home recipe. Just whip an ordinary stolid citizen into a country house, mix well with carpenters, painters and electricians, and in six hours he will be reduced to the consistency of a plate of warm calf's-foot jelly.

I slunk into my badger hole in the Keystone State some years ago with a couch hammock, an apparatus for making carbonated water which exploded, and a theory which exploded even more quickly. The theory was that I would lie in the hammock under the collected works of H. D. Thoreau and breathe gently through my gills until sleep knitted up the raveled sleave of care. For exercise, I planned to raise to my lips at regular intervals a small vase of fruit juice laced with gin and banked by fronds. My blueprints also called for a deep-bosomed mammy in snowy-white kerchief, who would issue from her laboratory every few minutes and revive my flagging strength with delicate little *canapés*, spoon bread and apple pandowdy.

I was still fuming over the knots in the hammock when a virago, played by my wife, entered intoning a dirge. The closets were too shallow for her evening gowns; the original Pennsylvania Dutch settlers had neglected to provide a glassed-in conservatory; she needed a special room with running water for washing dishes. Employing the simplest words, I patiently explained that I was not Diamond Jim Brady. With silken insolence, this starveling whom I had rescued from a taxi dance hall confided that, on the contrary, I usually reminded her of Uriah Heep or Old Scrooge. An instant later she regretted her tartness and, after applying beefsteak to her eye, I issued a writ for the necessary artisans.

For a month nobody appeared; then, one morning about four, I awoke to find myself in the midst of Donnybrook Fair. A well digger's derrick had sprung up at the foot of my bed and was boring toward China at two dollars a minute. Masons, plumbers, and tinsmiths swarmed through the rooms, wrestling and playing leapfrog. One gang of carpenters had peeled off the roof like the skin of an onion and was beating the rafters with mallets; a second was hurriedly erecting a scaffold to afford a better view of the maid in her shower. I had a slight headache caused by exposure to

some poisoned bourbon and the tumult made me rest-
less. I arose and, draped in a torn seersucker bathrobe,
fell downstairs over a scantling. Two jubilant carpenters awaited me.

"We're all out of cotter pins," they giggled,
"and you forgot the side anchors for the sash bolting."
I stuffed a shirt into a pair of pants and drove in my
robe to Bethlehem, thirty miles away. A canvass of five
hardware stores proved fruitless, but a few miles far-
ther, at Easton, I succeeded in picking up some cheap
sterling-silver bolts answering the purpose. The carpenters interrupted their rubber of bridge to examine
my purchase. "You should of brought the bronze
ones," they observed critically. "But we don't need 'em,
anyway. We used an old piece of baling wire."

At the close of business that evening they presented me with two gables of the original dwelling and
the second finest collection of pre-Revolutionary rub-
ble, banana-peels and waxed paper in North America.
I bedded down my flock in the grape arbor and lived
on potato chips for the duration. I paid the final bill
from an armored car escorted by six burly guards. The
varnish was scarcely dry on the floors when a friend
dropped in to see me. As I showed him proudly

through the house, he nodded appreciatively. "You've got a dandy layout here, old man," he admitted. "Why don't you shell out a few bucks and remodel it?"

NINE

According to recent figures compiled by trained statisticians working under filtered oatmeal, the first thing ninety-four per cent of the population does on acquiring a country place is to build some sort of swimming pool. The other six per cent instantly welshes on the deal and stops payment. I tried to, but the previous owner beat me to the bank. My checkbook had hardly ceased thrashing about in its final agony before I was out in whipcord breeches and cordovans, barking orders at a team of mules and a scoop shovel. I didn't want anything showy, just a fjord about the size of Lake Huron deep enough to float a yawl. In my overheated imagination I saw our anemic little creek transformed into a crystal mirror bordered by gay cabañas. I could almost hear the bevy of Powers models sighing with envy as my tanned, muscular form flashed off the springboard in a perfect swan dive. I even wired the Department of the Interior that if Grand Coulee proved insufficient, I could furnish water power to keep the wheels turning for a year or two.

What I had when the gang of workmen departed was a small, shrunken buffalo wallow infested with every variety of poisonous snake known to man, including several found only in the upper reaches of the Orinoco. Its surface was covered with an attractive green film dotted with decaying stumps and half-submerged oil cans. At night a dense mist shrouded the tarn; eerie lights flickered in the rushes, ghostly chuckles were audible, and if you ventured too close, you were liable to encounter a transparent citizen carrying his head under his arm. Thirteen families of ground hogs had set up light housekeeping in the dam itself, a massive affair of earth and logs that looked like the Union breastworks before Vicksburg. Every time it rained, the water boiled up, punching another hole in the structure, and I ran down the valley to pay the neighbors for the chickens it swept away. My children went hungry and unshod while I poured tons of cement into the coffers to make them hold. One morning I caught myself cackling hysterically and ramming an old mattress into the dam, and I knew I was licked. I called in the local dynamiter, indicated the project with a careless wave, and commanded him to erase it from the face of the earth.

The moment word was bruited about that Loch Wampum was doomed, the local savants gathered on the banks for a gleeful death watch. The man who had done the excavating was especially triumphant. "I could have told him it wouldn't work," he crowed. "By rights he should have dug out that gully where they dump the swill. Good stone bottom there." I asked him why he hadn't mentioned it earlier. "It don't pay to poke your nose in other people's business," he replied virtuously.

It took a day and a half for the dynamiter to drill the charges and string red flags across the township. On the appointed morning, the place was busier than New London during the Harvard-Yale regatta. Whole clans of Mennonites and Amish bearing lunch boxes arrived from the back country in ancient buckboards. Sightseers wandered through the garden poking sly fun at our vegetables, and one bystander mimicked my gait and speech so cleverly that I could not help sharing the general merriment. When everything was ready, I retired to the tool shed with my family and made them lie flat on the floor. With a warning, "Stand clear, all!" the dynamiter threw his switch. The blast which followed tore the roof off the springhouse and broke windows in the county seat sixteen miles away. Its only effect on the dam, however, was to harden the cement in it. My specialist bit his lip in chagrin. "I must have cut her a bit too fine," he confessed; "I'll fix her tomorrow, by cracky."

He kept his word. When the dust finally settled, I had enough firewood for the next fifty years, most of it right inside the house where I could get at it. And when *I* finally settled, the man next door had a new front porch and a glass eye you couldn't tell from the other one. Of course it's a bit unwieldy for five people to take a bath in a washtub, particularly at one time, but at least you don't have to look out for copperheads.

TEN

Years before I bought Rising Gorge, my Bucks County Chalet, I used to run into some former friend in a railroad terminal, his arms bristling with garden tools, insecticides and poultry leaflets, and a pair of rose-colored bifocals askew on his nose. Invariably the exile would sashay into a sales talk. "You owe it to the kiddies, old man," he would entreat, choking back a lump in his throat. "Never saw such a change in mine. Junior grew fourteen inches the first week. He's only nine, and he can split a cord of wood, milk twenty-one cows and cultivate a field of corn by sunup. Sister's not even three, but you ought to taste her preserves. They're famous for a hundred miles around."

In time the refrain began to worry me. I felt inferior on my son's third birthday that other men his age were operating combines when he could hardly shoe a horse. It humiliated me profoundly that my daughter, a strapping hulk of two, was unable to bake a pie. This process of slow erosion had its effect; one

Rising Gorge

morning I awoke with a dizzy feeling to find that I had acquired a piece of loam about the size of Nepal as a proving ground for their talents.

At first, in the natural bustle of making the house unlivable, the children were forgotten. Everything had to be scraped down to the original knotty pine, good hardware replaced with rusty hinges, wagon wheels substituted for candelabra, and the place generally made to resemble a rathskeller on the verge of bankruptcy. During this period a nurse stood guard over the brood, a sinister gargoyle with the temper of a wasp and a face hewn out of Indiana lime-stone. Miss Bramble had lived on some of the finest estates at Newport and had certain standards, even if she *was* working for poor white trash. Every afternoon she dressed her charges in Eton jackets, starched muslin, and velvet ribbons, which seemed rather formal wear for the manure pile. By skillful suggestion, she built up the notion of snakes in the greenery to the point where screams rang out when a salad was placed on the table. Her martydom reached a climax, however, at the sight of the master carrying ashes out of the cellar. She observed tartly that her late employer at Bailey's Beach had two foreigners to do that type of

work, both of whom were better groomed than myself.
I stood it until the children started following me
around with a chant Nanny had taught them. "Here
comes that ole ash man!" they jeered. "Any rags, any
bones, any bottles today?" I caught the pair of them
hiding in a drain and Nanny caught the 5:15.

For a month afterward, the hardy young pio-
neers refused to leave the kitchen. The yard, they
moaned, was full of great fur-bearing vampires with
human faces on the order of Miss Bramble's. Squealing,
kicking and gouging, they were flung outside each

morning, only to spend the day baying through the screen door. At length I made an eloquent speech painting the joys of a country childhood, embroidered with references to Huck Finn, slingshots, Barlow knives and fishing for bullheads. In closing, I presented the boy with a bamboo pole and a bent pin. With instinctive gallantry, the little chap promptly presented it to his sister, in the left eye. Giving him a kindly pat with a hairbrush, I changed my approach. I cited young Abe Lincoln, young Tom Edison, and other movie notables distinguished for their self-reliance. I explained how a poor youth named Benjamin Franklin had arrived in a great city munching a roll and had subsequently discovered the secret of electricity. My plea to emulate his example at once bore fruit. An hour later the porch was strewn with several half-eaten rolls and someone had short-circuited the wiring by forcing a key into a floor plug.

By now, of course, their dexterity and knowledge of country lore is fabulous; they have learned to perform a thousand disagreeable chores around the house. If I need a bean bag dropped into the plumbing to tie up the water system or tacks spread in the driveway so the tires take hold, I can count on the services

ELEVEN

Almost every Monday morning from May through late October, the Delaware Valley is the scene of a lovely old Pennsylvania Dutch ritual, or passion play, centering around my hovel. It is called "the changing of the maid," and, for sheer drama, suspense and production, far surpasses the changing of the guard at Buckingham Palace. It begins just about dawn with a salvo of saucepans and a poignant oratorio by the current cook. In this composition, the singer portrays herself as a sweet, patient foundling held prisoner by a drunken ogre who compels her to wear shoes while serving and sleep in a room with windows. Its climax is a haunting cadenza representing the boss as a tyrant, a miser and a leech. Soon a deeper baritone voice blends in with a ballad entitled "If We Can Do Without Broadway, We Can Do Without You." Following a brisk andante movement of a fountain pen scratching out a reference, a colorful procession winds toward the garage—the squire in his purple pajamas, with face to match, and behind him a grim domestic muttering to her satchels. As the screech of the gears fades into the distance, the brief tinkle of a telephone dialing a New York employment agency rings down the curtain.

No country home is complete without a surly figure seated in the kitchen like Rodin's Thinker, wishing she was back in a hot little room under the Third Avenue Elevated. Any maid who leaves the city is either suffering from a nervous breakdown or hiding from the Feds, which amounts to the same thing. Most of the ones I employed during the last decade wore a hunted look and carried hatboxes containing powerful short-wave radios. The moment the dishes were done, they would race to their rooms to broadcast our menu and other vital defense secrets to the Wilhelmstrasse. The last one always hummed the Horst Wessel song as she passed the mashed potatoes. She left in a fury when I refused to celebrate Hitler's birthday with a lawn party.

Perhaps the sorriest sight on a rural-free-delivery route is the transplanted jitterbug. Early this semester I imported a tense, wild-eyed creature named Rhodesia whose sole baggage was a make-up kit and a pair of dance clogs. Her face fell as we pulled away from the station. "I don't see no Ferris wheel," she whimpered. "The missus tole me you lived right smack on the midway." I explained that our farm was only three miles from a bustling village of fifty souls and that a neighbor's lights were clearly visible on the next ridge. Passing her tongue over her parched lips, she ventured the opinion that the region was full of wild animals. I quickly reassured her that apart from an occasional werewolf, days would elapse without her seeing a sign of life. She spent the balance of the trip alternately caressing a rabbit's foot and consulting the

Witch's Dream Book. On arriving at the hacienda, she hid under the porch for two hours, just because one of the dogs had romped with her throat. Dinner that night was fried chicken Maryland style, featuring pin feathers and a dash of coffee grounds. My wife offered her a book to take to bed, but she chose a cleaver instead. In the morning she showed her true colors by spitefully alluding to the maid's room as a chicken coop—pure malice, since no chickens had lived in it for more than a year and it had had a heavy coat of whitewash. Her dream book, she added, predicted a calamity unless she left at once. I had obtained the same prediction by simply studying the oatmeal, and in a trice Rhodesia was free, reasonably white, and twenty-one.

A series of local girls ranging from twelve to fifteen pitched out the fodder for a while thereafter, but there was always a rawboned suitor guffawing in the kitchen and shrill squeals of "Stop tickling me!" at mealtime. After eating a bran muffin in which the chef had also included scratch feed and oats, I wired New York for a really competent couple. The next morning, while I was processing a load of fertilizer in front of the barn, a long black Mercedes drew up bearing two poised and gracious gentlefolk. They examined the place attentively. "This is the gatekeeper's lodge," the woman said in Italian. "Ask this peasant where the main house is." I touched my cap, indicated the woods, and I haven't seen them since. My wife looks pretty tacky in a Mother Hubbard and you can get tired of turnips, but give me home cooking every time.

TWELVE

Now that spring again weaves a nest of robins in my hair and the first installment of the income tax fades into a discolored bruise, that annual bugbear, the vegetable garden, arises to plague me. As one who achieved the symmetry of a Humphrey Bogart and the grace of a jaguar purely on pastry, I have no truck with lettuce, cabbage and similar chlorophyll. Any dietitian

will tell you that a running foot of apple strudel contains four times the vitamins of a bushel of beans. In
my own case, at least, greens are synonymous with
poison. Every time I crunch a stalk of celery, there is a
whirring crash, a shriek of tortured capillaries, and my
metabolism goes to the boneyard. Yet come the middle
of April, the family invariably gets an urge to see the
old man beating his brains out in the garden patch. It's
funny, but nobody ever gets an urge to see him snooz-
ing on the lounge. If he isn't staggering under a wheelbarrow of manure or grubbing in the subsoil, he's a
leper.

Planning a garden takes place, as all the handbooks advise, long before the frost is out of the ground, preferably on a night recalling Keats's "Eve of St. Agnes," with hail lashing the windows. The dependents reverently produce the latest seed catalogue and succumb to mass hypnosis. "Look at those radishes— two feet long!" everyone marvels. "We could have them, too, if that lazy slug didn't curl up in the hammock all day." A list of staples is speedily drawn up: Brussels sprouts the size of a rugby, eggplant like captive balloons, and yams. Granny loves corn fritters; a half acre is allotted to Golden Bantam. The children need a pumpkin for Halloween, and let's have plenty of beets, we can make our own lump sugar. Then someone discovers the hybrids—the onion crossed with a pepper or a new vanilla-flavored turnip that plays the "St. James Infirmary Blues." When the envelope is finally sealed, the savings account is a whited sepulcher and all we need is a forty-mule team to haul the order from the depot.

The moment the trees are in bud and the soil is ready to be worked, I generally come down with a crippling muscular complaint as yet unclassified by science. Suffering untold agonies, I nonetheless have myself wheeled to the side line and coach a small, gnarled man of seventy in the preparation of the seedbed. The division of labor works out perfectly; he spades, pulverizes and rakes the ground, while I call out encouragement and dock his pay whenever he straightens up to light his pipe. The relationship is an ideal one, and I know he will never leave me as long as the chain remains fastened to his leg.

Within a few weeks the plants are sturdily poking their heads through the lava and broken glass, just in time to be eaten by cutworms, scorched by drought and smothered by weeds. The weeds native to the Pennsylvania countryside surpass in luxuriance anything you would encounter in the jungles of Cochin China or French Equatorial Africa. One variety I raised last summer had the sly hangdog phiz of a bookie and whispered off-color jokes every time I passed. Another, a revolting little fat weed, possessed the power of locomotion; it used to sneak around like Pecksniff, as though butter wouldn't melt in its mouth. I was also successful in developing a curious man-eating snail; but when the news photographer arrived to get a close-up, he and the snail frightened each other off the premises.

By the end of August the residue left by the rabbits and woodchucks is ready for harvest. It is always the same—tomatoes and squash. Tomatoes and squash never fail to reach maturity. You can spray them with acid, beat them with sticks and burn them; they love it. In forty-eight hours the place is knee-deep in rotting pulp and a fearful miasma overhangs the valley. Soon the most casual acquaintances start dropping by with creaking baskets and hypocritical smiles, attempting to fob off their excess tomatoes and squash. The more desperate even abandon tiny bundles on our doorstep like infants at the House of the Good Shepherd. The kitchen becomes an inferno of steam and the wife a frenzied sorceress stirring caldrons of pink slush. Ultimately, with a fanfare comparable to launching a dreadnought, two minute jars filled with an appalling green emulsion are brought to the table. If you don't taste it, you're a cad; if you do, you're a cadaver. The only solution is to plow everything under and live on pie. Reach for the sky, partner; I'm the Crisco Kid.

THIRTEEN

Look, friends, I'm just an ordinary country boy. I'm slow, and sort of quizzical, and as plain as an old board fence. I prize the quiet, homely things—applejack out of a charred keg, a bundle of faded securities, the rustle of old greenbacks. I love the scent of fresh-mown clover and the giggles that escape from it on a warm summer afternoon. But what I value most is solitude. Years ago, before I renounced the topless towers of Manhattan and settled in the bush, I couldn't get my fill of revelry. When the drummer was stowing away his traps and the last couples lingered in Flirtation Row, I was still dancing the camel walk and the balconade. Today I'm a deep-dish hermit. I'd like to see anyone get *me* into a hot, noisy night club filled with people eating synthetic chow mein and leering at young persons in their frillies. Yes, sir, I want to see him try. My telephone number is Buckwheat 489-Ring 3, and I'll be wearing my tuxedo, just in case.

If rural life has done anything, it has taught me to be self-sufficient; I pity a man who can't be alone. There is nothing like a solitary evening in an old house, cooped up with one's dogs and books, to sharpen the senses and shorten the wind. One night recently, for instance, I suddenly felt I had to think things out and packed my family off to the seashore. It was ten above zero and building to a blizzard, but when I have to think things out I have no time for sentimental considerations. Breathing a sigh of relief, I double-locked the doors, barricaded them with bureaus and chairs, and set about preparing supper. I had some difficulty getting the beans out of the can, but I shortly contrived a serviceable bandage for my wrist and snuggled down in front of a crackling fire with the diaries of Wilfred Scawen Blunt. I had read little more than three pages when I realized I was holding the diaries upside down and listening intently to a noise in the kitchen.

Loosely speaking, the sound combined a creak and a sigh suggestive of a musical saw. Now and again, it was smothered by a soft, mirthless laugh ending in a sharp click. My dogs, quick to guard their master, formed into a hollow square and withdrew under the couch. I dried my palms, which seemed to have accumulated a slight film of oil, and picked up the fire tongs. "Who's there?" I inquired in a crisp falsetto. (After all, I thought, why waste a trip to the kitchen if nobody was there?) There was no answer; whoever it was didn't even have the common decency to reply. Angered, I strode toward the kitchen, whistling to warn of my approach, and flung open the door. Everything was in apple-pie order, including the apple pie, except that the rocking chair was bobbing slowly back and forth.

"That's odd—very odd," I murmured, re-entering the living room and tripping over a chair. "Probably caused by a draft from an open window or something."

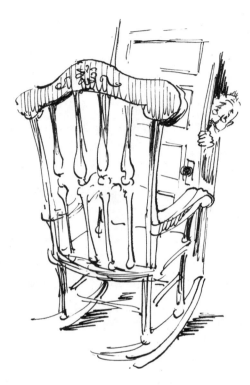

"Or something," agreed one of the dogs from under the couch.

"Who said that?" I demanded sharply. The craven cur was frightened back into silence. I yawned casually, an effort that almost resulted in lockjaw, and consulted my watch. "Well, guess I'll turn in," I observed to nobody in particular. Hearing no objection, I started for the stairs, the dogs clustered about my ankles. A brisk, affable voice cut me short.

"The three homicidal maniacs who fled the county home for the insane are still at large tonight," it said chattily. "If you see a burly man of fifty with an ice pick—" I cannot abide petty gossip; switching off the radio, I went up the steps, taking them four at a time. It was a trifle close under the covers, especially as the dogs persisted in huddling in with me, but it made for a warm, *gemütlich* feeling. About 9:30, someone in the attic started dragging a body across the floor by the hair, occasionally belting it with a strap. My blood boiled at the cruelty, and yet it occurred to me it was really none of my affair. I had lived in the house only eleven years; the people upstairs were undoubtedly the pre-Civil War tenants, who had every right to do as they pleased. I took ten or twelve small fruit tablets and straightway fell into a refreshing doze, which would have lasted until morning had my family not returned unexpectedly. They had a little trouble recognizing me with white hair, although otherwise I was the same kindly, indulgent Dads they had always worshipped. In a way, it was fun seeing them, too, but one of these days I've simply got to get away by myself and think things out.

FOURTEEN

If you tossed a cigarette out of a plane thirty
minutes west of LaGuardia Airport, it would
probably hit the roof of an enormous red barn
decorated with hex symbols, and, just between
you and me and the compost, that would be okay
with me. For the past fifteen years, until a week
ago, this hippodrome served superficially as a
receptacle for old newspapers and fly screens,

but actually as the focus of a dream. Whenever I was pressed to convert it into a studio, playroom or summer theater—one man tried to rent it for a stocking factory—I assumed a crafty, slow-witted, peasant's smile. In my mind's eye I saw the stalls lined with sleek purebreds gorging themselves on alfalfa, the great silo bursting with high-protein hay. To my fevered senses, no imported perfume could rival the bouquet of a heifer placidly chewing her cud. Every moment I wasn't sleeping, I greedily devoured government bulletins detailing the manufacture of smearcase and clabber. I could almost hear the rich golden milk gurgling in the pails; I grew faint with desire picturing myself at eventide in the north forty, surrounded by lowing kine.

I could have gone on dreaming indefinitely, without ever disbursing a kopeck, had it not been for Lowing Klein, the advertising man next door. For some obscure reason, this worthy unexpectedly tired of feeding a hundred and forty pedigreed Jerseys and put them under the hammer. Trumpeting the historic phrase, "I'm just looking for a small family cow," I donned my most evil-smelling tweeds and raced to the auction. It was held under a striped marquee crowded with scores of fellow poets and playwrights also avid for a small family cow. Interspersed in the throng were members of the best county families leaning on shooting sticks and surveying one another insolently. As I arrived, a cow roughly the size of the frigate "Constitution" was led into the tanbark ring. The two brawny stable hands petting her seemed pygmies.

"Zangwill's Bijou Lass," droned the auctioneer, "the daughter of Throaty Contralto by that great sire Glittering Generalization, seven times winner over the Isle of Jersey." The bidding soared dizzily to three hundred and ten dollars, languished and died. Suddenly a voice I dimly recognized as my own squeaked, "Three hundred and twenty!" I turned pale with terror, knowing full well I didn't own three hundred and twenty of anything, let alone the artistic pale green rugs issued by the Treasury Department. Before I could extricate myself, the auctioneer had brought me to my knees and was administering the *estocada.* In vain I pleaded I had merely been clearing my throat, that I lived in a hotel for business girls where no cattle were permitted, and that I was a small-time grifter currently under indictment for passing bad checks. With a cold nod signifying I was united in holy matrimony to twelve hundred pounds of brisket, the auctioneer swept on to another item. Two awed yokels nearby eyed me respectfully. "That's Bet-a-Million Titus," I overheard them whispering. "They claim his place is bigger than the King Ranch in Texas." The compliment acted on me like adrenaline; in the next ten minutes I snapped up a towering jumbo with an annual record of two thousand pounds of butterfat, and a trim gazelle reputed to yield sixteen quarts of Devonshire clotted cream at a milking.

By the time I returned home, my giddiness had subsided, leaving me weak and trembling with remorse. I was maundering through an incredible fable about having won a calf at a raffle when a van puffed up the incline bearing my moolies. My dream girl turned a dusty vermilion and uttered a choking sound. I offered to explain to her how milking would strengthen her fingers and broaden her psyche, but the poor creature, irrational as only her sex can be, caught up a nest of flowerpots and was trying to get my range. I spent the night doubled up in a feed bin, listening to the mammoths eating me into bankruptcy and endlessly adding up columns of figures. To date, they have tucked away twelve bales of hay, five blocks of salt and three bushels of a mealy substance weighed out on

FIFTEEN

Is anybody around here looking for a bargain in an Early Pennsylvania washstand in mint condition, circa 1825? It is genuine pumpkin pine, with ball-and-claw feet, the original brasses, and a small smear of blood where I tripped over it last night in the dark. I am holding it at sixteen dollars, but not so tightly that I wouldn't let it go to the right party for circa ten cents. I also have an authentic trestle table which collapses into a small space when you merely rest your elbows on it, and a patchwork quilt I bought from a very old lady who remembered seeing Lincoln. She must have seen P.T. Barnum as well, for I heard her observe to her husband that there was one born every minute. In fact, I am disposing of my entire collection of antiques to the lowest bidder, and if he doesn't want it, I intend to set fire to it as soon as I can find an Early American match.

When, back in the mid-thirties, I left a cozy New York flat to exile myself in a stone pillbox in a swamp, I broke clean with the twentieth century. I was ready to dip candles and card my own flax if need be, and the thought of profaning our primitive farmhouse with Grand Rapids furniture made me shudder. I promptly installed a spinning wheel in every room, in case anyone should need some quick homespun, and replaced our luxurious inner-spring bed with a period four-poster. My neighbor hesitated to relinquish it at first, as it had been serving as a roost for his chickens, but finally exchanged it for five acres of prime bottom land. Another party graciously consented to trade our priceless Bokhara carpets for a small hooked rug he had won playing ski-ball at the Lancaster Fair. I even discarded the electric stove and returned to cooking in the fireplace, until my wife, with typical feminine squeamishness, ran a temperature because a couple of grilled tomtits turned up in the soup one evening.

In spite of all our efforts, the house still seemed bourgeois and prosaic. The lamps gave off too much light and the bureau drawers worked too easily. We lusted for lamps made out of old seltzer bottles or apothecaries' jars, and Victorian dressers that nobody could open. One day on a back road near Prosaic, New Jersey, we stumbled into a web run by a spider named Jake Meserve. Outwardly Jake was a farmer; he had a long linen duster, steel-bowed spectacles, and a field of papier-mâché corn in front of his place as a blind. In his hayloft, however, he kept a few choice heirlooms you could persuade him to sell by dropping your hat. We immediately fell in love with a rare old cobbler's bench, as fine a piece as you would find outside the Metropolitan—that is, the Metropolitan Shoe Repair Shop. After a brisk tussle, Jake stowed my thirty-nine dollars in a poke next to his skin and hauled out a rickety sofa specked with mildew.

"You folks ever seen a real old-time Victorian courtin' chair?" he inquired, stroking the plush. "I mind my Uncle Zeb proposed to Aunt Mildew in that chair. I wouldn't part with it if I was starvin'." Suddenly he choked back a sob and turned away. "Take it," he muttered brokenly. "Ninety-three dollars. It's like sellin' my own flesh and blood."

I whittled him down to sixty in a trice, and drying his eyes, he disgorged three more family mementos—a dough tray, a glass bell containing his mother's baby hair, and a little chest of drawers lettered, "Willimantic Spool & Thread Co." He stripped my wallet of everything but the social-security card and we embarked. As I threw the car into gear, he staggered up, bearing a gate-leg table.

"Just ran acrost this in my feed bin," he panted. "My grandpa bought it off Nancy Hanks. You can scrape off the paint with a stiff brush."

I threw him my watch and chain, and we whizzed away. I spent the next week hacking at the table with a blowtorch, steel wool, and sandpaper. It had six coats of paint, including one like porcelain that had been baked on. When I had finished, I overturned it accidentally and discovered a sticker reading, "R.H. Macy & Co. Reduced to $3.98." And that, children, is how daddy met his first psychiatrist.

SIXTEEN

If you happen to be lolling around Penn Station of a Friday afternoon and see a sullen couple vaguely resembling crocodiles, carrying tennis rackets and boxes of cheap candy, you can make book that they are weekend guests bound for my pleasure dome in Tinicum Township. I don't know what alchemy there is about those railroad stations, but Jekyll and Hyde aren't in it. I have had staunch lifelong friends, the kind of people you swap neckties with, start down the escalator, chortling in anticipation of my hospitality, and reach the train embittered old crabs, loudly beefing about the service, the beds and the liquor, though they were seventy miles from it. Possibly the railroad maintains some devilish kind of decompression chamber, like that used by sand hogs, to temper my guests. If so, it needs one added operation, in which the candidate is given a hang-over and a case of ptomaine, infested with wood ticks, and shot out into Seventh Avenue, free to spend the weekend his own way. This would also allow me time for my own work, which is to lie doggo until noon and compose jeremiads about country living.

I was a week-end guest, too, before my favorite cat died and willed me eighteen million dollars, but I remember myself as a sweet, patient duck whom host-esses would give their right eye to entertain—and if you don't think so, just look at the scores of one-eyed hostesses you meet nowadays. The moment I left the bread line and opened my own soup kitchen, however, a bunch of parasites invaded the field. It's not the money that bothers me, mind you; it's the principle of the thing.

Whether I meet them at the railhead personally or dispatch my Chinese houseboy with his rickshaw, they are disgruntled from the start. "Some railroad," they snarl. "Can't even get Pojarski cutlets and wild rice in the diner." Judging from the striped blazers, ski trousers, and fur-lined parkas they descend in, they must think they are visiting Lake Placid or the Laurentians. One man arrived in mid-September with a toboggan and a set of racing blades. He was furious because the Delaware & Lackawanna had no accommodations for his malemutes. When he found no ice in the creek, he flew into a paroxysm. "What the hell is this, the bayou country?" he shouted. "I spent a dollar thirty-eight getting to this hothouse!" I offered him the address of an igloo on West Forty-fifth Street that served a good grade of blubber, but he grudgingly consented to stay and cadge a few meals.

En route to the leprosarium, I customarily make a short historical talk, indicating the covered bridge where Simon Flannel deployed his men to counter the Hessian thrust, the local Lover's Leap, and the like. Such details enchant city people, and they always inquire, "What do you do for French vermouth down here?" They generally begin to get drowsy as we ford the creek below the farm, and by dinner time Cheyne-Stokes breathing has set in. Since the cook invariably quits at the sight of company, my vixen has to don burnt cork and a turban, but they pinch her with the same easy familiarity they display to all domestics. A certain elderly wolf, undismayed by a cuff on the bugle, even offered her fifty cents to rub his back, pleading that his wife was a hopeless invalid who never really understood him in the first place.

Once the victuals are down, the female waddles painfully to the nearest sofa and collapses, while the male points out little errors of construction I have made around the place. At nine, both retire to bed with a bottle and our honeyed entreaties to sleep as long as they like. In less time than it takes to read *Henry Esmond*, the dishes are washed, cigarettes dug out of the veneer, and we are in bed listening to them giggling through the partition over our stinginess.

About the cocktail hour next day, after our house has rung to reverberating snores like the beat of surf at Coronado, two somnambulists appear and waspishly demand farina, plovers' eggs and Canadian bacon. Any attempt to drag them outdoors is futile; they've seen all the grass they care to in Central Park.

They are still in pajamas when the local gentry bursts in, crying, like Cynara's lover, for madder music and stronger wine. From then on, the evening is a montage of broken glassware, stolen embraces, and recriminations. At the grim-lipped caucus on the platform Sunday night, the delegates display a copper nimbus around the skull and undying hatred for each other. Well, here we are, boy. Call me up when you get to town, boy. You bet I will, boy. Now take it easy, boy. And don't drop dead before I see you, boy.

SEVENTEEN

Somewhere in the South Atlantic, off the charted ship lanes, there is thought to be a vast turgid eddy known as the Sargasso Sea, in which the derelicts of the seven seas ultimately come to rest. (My authority for the foregoing is a noted oceanographer named Turgid Eddie whom I met in a small West Side laboratory a few days ago and who drank nothing but Scotch and sea water.) Now this theory is all very well for schoolgirls and neurotic women, but the actual Sargasso is nowhere near the South Atlantic. It is situated in half a quarter section of rolling scrub midway between New York and Philadelphia, and embodies the worst features of both. At its core stands the shabby-genteel spokesman of these lines, slowly shedding his sanity as a terrifying vortex of dogs, debts and petty afflictions swirls sluggishly about his knees.

I might have dragged out my days in our gravel pit in peace, a myopic bookworm in sleeve garters and an alpaca jacket content to fuss among his ageratum, but for a remark of my wife's. It ran: "Couldn't we afford a dog, dear? It'd keep me company while you're in town chasing around with those doxies of yours." Quick to humor a poor woman's whim, I drove the poor little soul to a roadside kennel that was closing out a job lot of pets. I soon found the ideal companion for her, a ten-cent turtle bearing the legend, "Greetings from Savin Rock," but the willful creature must begin haggling over a chow with the proprietor, a shifty freebooter with only one eye. He could see well enough out of the other, however, to distinguish the bulge of my wallet, toward which he swung constantly, like the needle of a compass.

"You don't find them dogs every day," he told us confidentially. "That pup was stolen from one of the finest homes in Germantown." Aware that any show of feeling would increase the price, my wife cunningly betrayed her indifference by cradling the animal in her arms and covering his muzzle with kisses. The ruse worked, and we got him for only ninety dollars, less than the average man spends a month on Gutenberg Bibles.

It took nearly an hour for Wang's initial shyness to wear off. The last of it disappeared at the general store as motherly old Mrs. Sigafoos bent over him to coo an endearment. With a sibilant hiss, he tore the fichu from her blouse and she fell into a display of fig bars. A hearty laugh and a dizzying bribe quickly restored good spirits, and we set off for home. En route, we stopped briefly at the villa of an artist neighbor for a cup of hot milk and grenadine. The door was opened by Mrs. van Gogh, modishly clad in a new hostess gown for the occasion, bearing a Siamese cat in her arms. Wang joyfully blew battle stations, and Grimalkin, employing his mistress as a Jacob's Ladder, hastily went topside and lodged in her coiffure. Over

the iodine and gauze we all became fast friends, and I
even bought a dry point from them which I needed like
a hole in the head. My wife still insists I kept referring
to it as a blue point, but of course she was somewhat
unnerved.

For the next two days you would never have
known there was a dog on the place, apart from the
occasional stifled cry as Wang's teeth closed on a child.
His daily routine was almost Spartan: in the morning
a rapid round of the local garbage piles, at noon a
casual lunch of two or three stray pullets, and toward

sundown a vigorous uprooting of our shrubs. Thanks to this rigid discipline, he was trained to razor edge for his farewell performance. The setting was the porch and his co-star a schnauzer imported by a fair week-end guest. In the heat of the struggle, milady felt it best to thrust her foot between the actors. Wang, ever a boy with a sweet tooth, started stuffing himself, and it required a spirited massage with a bone-handled umbrella to distract the glutton. The hushed calm that ensued was broken only by the crackle of a crisp bank note and a deep sigh.

I traded Wang for a collie who brought home skunks, and turned Laddie Boy in for a Kerry who ate maids. At last, in desperation, I bought a bloodhound, a timid thing with great gentle eyes like a fawn. The man swore she was barely able to walk, much less attack anybody. A fortnight later, she knocked down a state trooper, stole his pistol, and held up a cigar store in Doylestown. And if you don't believe me, ask her brother. He's working for the Bureau of Internal Revenue.

EIGHTEEN

A few days back, while waiting around my
doctor's anteroom to have a swelling
excised from my checkbook, I ran across an
extremely informative article in a medical jour-
nal named *Peeping Tom* or *Hot Dickety*—at
least, that was the name on the leather binder. A
well-known physician, writing under the nom de
plume of Chicken Inspector No. 23, had made a

comparative study of ten New York women with an equal number of outlanders to determine which group was healthier. As all the subjects examined turned out to be lightly-draped showgirls, those who were stunted or undernourished were immediately obvious to the reader. The conclusions were unmistakable: the city girls had glossy pelts and eyes sparkling with fun, whereas their country cousins were torpid and lackluster. So once again the rosy fiction that country living is wholesome has been disproved. If anyone wants to trade a couple of centrally-located, well-cushioned showgirls for an eroded slope ninety minutes from Broadway, I'll be on this corner tomorrow at eleven with my tongue hanging out.

There is probably no more striking illustration of the change wrought by life in the canebrake than my own case. When I first took to the hills, I was a sad apology for a man. Reared on goose cracklings, rich sauces, and liqueur Scotch, I was practically on the verge of collapse. My teeth had achieved a dreary uniformity from excessive dental care and my skin was worn parchment-thin from too much bathing. My system cried out for plain, honest country fare— skimmed milk, margarine, and macaroni. After six months in the tall rhubarbs, I was a new man. My cheeks developed the ruddy vitality of a pail of lard and my fingers were permanently knotted with arthritis. I had all the allergies of Marcel Proust without any of the talent. My life-insurance beneficiaries discussed me openly in the past tense. The more charitable held that I had been a mean little skinflint who might surprise everybody when the will was finally probated.

It was not until I fell afoul of two local doctors, however, that I got my comeuppance. The first was a small, sallow practitioner who had been graduated brilliantly from a mail-order institution a week previously and was waiting to recoup his tuition on the next stray patient. He was out in his back yard splitting a fee when I drove up. His face betrayed the stupefaction of a trapper who sees a sable walk into his snare. In a second, however, he recovered his poise, and barking his shins on a sawhorse to conceal his satisfaction, he swept me into the consulting room.

"That's a nasty throat you have there, brother," he jabbered before I could get my coat off. "Yes sirree, you've got tularemia if I ever saw it. And those adenoids'll have to come out along with the appendix. What did you say your bank was—I mean, your name?" I hurriedly explained that a hornet had stung me in the neck while I was pruning the lilacs and that all I required was a powder to relieve the headache. Thrusting a bronchoscope down my gullet, he cut short my case history.

"Your pancreas is full of tacks, mister," he reported. "Besides, there's a chicken bone lodged in your lung. Better let me have twenty dollars on account; you look sort of sneaky." By the time I regained the open air, he had taken a blood count, a hemoglobin sample, and all the loose change in my vest. He clung to the running board clawing at my stickpin, but an overhanging willow branch brushed him off. The last I heard as my car careened out into the highway was his frenzied promise to sue me for the balance of the bill.

The second prospector to tap the lode was a benevolent old healer, a horse-and-buggy doctor in the great tradition of Lionel Barrymore and Jean Hersholt. To furnish the authentic character touch, he parked his custom-built Packard phaeton at the foot of the lane and pulled up before my door in an ancient sleigh. I was lying abed with a dramatic wheeze and a temperature of 109. The thermometer he plunged into my mouth was encrusted with snuff, and I sneezed.

"What's the matter, got a cold or something?" he inquired, wiping a hypodermic on his coattails. "Here, this'll fix you up." I remonstrated timidly that there was a bit of rust on the needle; he grew scarlet with fury. "Germs, germs, germs!" he shouted. "Who feeds you that infernal poppycock? You can't *see* them, can you?" He advised a poultice of bacon rind, corn meal, and flannel, pocketed all the folding money in sight, and stormed out. That night I swelled up like a sunfish and went into acidotic coma. When I finally

reached New York in a solid silver ambulance inlaid with rubies, I found I had double pneumonia with complications. Which is a pretty understatement indeed for a house in the country.

NINETEEN

Not long ago, while waiting around Grand Central to have my pocket picked, I was approached by a rather dashing woman of the world with a request for a light. I am not one of those who kiss and tell, but, frankly, men, she was the bee's knees. Her general appearance suggested a younger Lillian Russell; she was dressed in skunk-dyed sable, had a sable-dyed skunk on a leash, and altogether resembled a yacht of the "Defender" class. Naturally, I was somewhat wary at first and nervously fingered the lunch money that mummy had pinned inside my jumper. I indicated a newsstand close by at which matches were being offered for sale, but my fair suppliant confessed the headmistress of her boarding school had cautioned her against strange newsstands. My innate chivalry rose to the surface, and I escorted her forthwith to a snug little *boite* where we could discuss her dilemma.

I mention the incident only because my wife boasted to a dinner party the other evening that I probably knew more tramps than any man alive—meaning, of course, that I knew more hobos. Scarcely a day passes on my demesne that some cheerful vagabond does not drop in for a handout and a flop. From Memphis to Mobile, from Natchez to St. Joe, wherever the cold winds blow, the name of "Cotton Ed" Perelman spells hospitality. As a matter of fact, I chose the farm for its proximity to three railroads and the Lincoln Highway; my money was multiplying at such a rate I was paying people to truck it away and burn it. I still have to scuff the greenbacks off my shoes before entering the house, but at least it's tidier than it was.

Though our clientele is usually a jovial, high-spirited lot, we occasionally draw some sourballs. Last Tuesday afternoon the vicomtesse and I were dawdling on the piazza when a couple of bindle stiffs appeared. The wayfarers had red putty noses, three-day beards, and bundles slung over their shoulders on peeled-willow wands. Tags attached to their lapels read "Weary Willie" and "Dusty Rhodes"; they were perspiring profusely and extremely irritable.

"Why, whoever are those dubious characters?" inquired my chatelaine, surveying them fastidiously through her lorgnette.

"Oh, just a couple of hot cross bums," I ventured. "Step in, gentlemen; this is your home away from home."

"Is dis de spot wit' de free grub?" one of them demanded suspiciously. I assured him it was and, reaching for the bell pull, bade Uncle Cudgo serve up his most savory repast. From the first mouthful, they proved petty and disagreeable. Brushing aside the cheese soufflé Aunt Hagar had prepared, they ordered her to place huckleberry pies to cool in the kitchen window so they might steal them. They turned up their noses at the coffee in our Sèvres-china cups, and, creating a replica of a hobo jungle in the living room, brewed mulligan stew and coffee in an old tin can. Their derision reached a peak when I offered them my downy feather bed.

"What's de matter, cul, ain't youse got a hay-mow?" they sneered. I conducted the pair to the barn, pressed a handful of five-cent stogies and a pail of canned heat on them, and begged them to sleep until the cows came home—the cows were at a Princeton house party that weekend. I then secreted myself behind a bag of mash to eavesdrop on their conversation.

"Dere's somethin' loony about. dis joint," I heard one mutter. "Dey ain't got no bulldog to bite youse in de seat o' yer pants." The other reassured him and, lighting their cigars, they settled down to ten minutes of rapid-fire tramp comedy.

"Say, Weary," said Dusty, "why is a hobo like a dentist?"

"Dey both live from hand ter mouth," riposted the other. "Say, Dusty, I went up to a lady dis mornin' and asked her fer some cold vittles."

"What did youse get?"

"De cold shoulder," returned Weary. "Say, Dusty, I read an absorbin' article in de paper today. It was about a sponge."

"Well, well, so dey been writin' up yer brudder again," Dusty remarked. "Say, Weary, one time I fell down a hill wit' ten bottles o' beer and didn't break one."

"Why was dat, kiddo?" his foil queried.

"'Cuz dey was inside o' me," Dusty chuckled. Thereupon they belabored each other with rolled-up newspapers, sang a chorus of "Pie in the Sky," and retired. The next morning I discovered to my chagrin that they had decamped without even rifling the henhouse, and, as a final gesture of contempt, had scrawled on the barn in chalk: "Stay away from dese rubes, men: dey're both dead beats." That's what you get for being an easy mark. I tell you, it's enough to shake your faith in humanity.

TWENTY

Next to drinking brandy before breakfast, the most fatal mistake a man can commit is to isolate himself in the country. In no time at all, he becomes broody and morose, a crosspatch and a mope. I avoided the pitfall by a simple device. A week before I bought my grange, I had just signed a three-year lease on a New York apartment—a bit of foresight still known in the family as "Mummy's First Stroke, or the Deerfield Massacre." Consequently, I now can run in every other week at my own expense to serve eviction papers, excavate the debris, and generally explain to the police why my tenants drop bags of water on passers-by. This stimulating exercise keeps my blood pressure in the upper brackets and results in what doctors call "tissue tone." It also results in what they call "insolvency"— the medical term for great hollow circles under the bank balance.

By shrewd selection, I have managed to saddle myself with some fairly spectacular saboteurs, male and female alike. One season I rented my flat to a breezy newspaperman who introduced himself as "Scoops" Conlon of the *Daily Planet.* While he was binding the bargain with a counterfeit money order, three brawny colleagues appeared, laden with cases of soda, lemons and cracked ice. He disclosed that they were his roommates and had been waiting outside until the deal was consummated. As I crossed the sidewalk to enter a cab, I narrowly escaped an empty bottle of rye. The next time I saw the premises, a month later, they looked as though a cavalry patrol headed by Jubal A. Early had bivouacked there for the night.

Somebody had built a bonfire in the bedroom and baked hoe-cakes in the ashes. What remained of the walls was redecorated with a sprightly series of anatomical studies done in indelible lipstick. Except for a semi-paralyzed stranger under the stove clutching a vial of Jamaica ginger, the place was as neat as a pen.

The following year my advertisement attracted the sweetest old lady in the world, with a lovely patrician head and a velvet choker. From the way her fingers caressed my books and symphony records, I could tell at once she was a connoisseur of the finer things. I asked her whether she liked poetry, of which I had a modest collection. "You're cookin' on the front burner, Mac," she returned hoarsely. "I always got my nose in a poem." I accepted a draft on a bank in Buenos Aires, and, in parting, she casually inquired where the nearest pawnshop was. I thought nothing of it at the time, nor did the superintendent when he saw my piano being moved out. "I figured your mother knew what she was doing," he told me. "Say, you've got a telephone bill for two hundred dollars."

The diggings stood vacant for a while, but by baiting the deadfall with a four-month concession, I

turned up a pair of extremely gifted girls. They knew
what they wanted and set out at once to achieve it with
the scant materials on hand. To begin with, they made
a trio of stunning low coffee tables by merely sawing
down the legs of the end tables. They then papered the
bedroom with a busy pattern of satyrs and dryads and
re-covered all the upholstery in bed ticking, using a
remnant as a skirt for the telephone. Everything in
sight was looped back on itself. As a final touch, they
pasted stars on all the mirrors. Apparently the experience went to their heads like May wine, for they ultimately glued them to the andirons, the bathtub and a
pair of shoes I had left in a closet. As I entered the foyer
with the marshal, the first thing I fell over was an iron
pickaninny in jockey costume holding a ring toward
me. The second thing I fell over was the lessees, sobbing
into a chalice of gin.

Last summer two sets of swallows roosted
briefly in my nest. One was an oily gentleman who
informed me he was a spice merchant. One evening the
Spice Squad broke in, took a gander at his wares, and
gave him a room rent-free for the next six months. The
other was a retired woodcarver who suddenly returned
to his trade, employing his wife as a medium. Next

spring I intend to be more particular. I'll consider a nice quiet family—that is, a family of bats.

TWENTY-ONE

For my money, the most parochial, unwholesome aspect of contemporary civilization is the life led by the average urban dweller. Cooped up in a stuffy, over-heated hotel suite with nothing but a bowl of cracked ice, a blonde, and a fleet bellboy poised on his toe like Pavlova waiting to run errands, he misses the rich, multiple savor of country living. He never knows the fierce ecstasy of rising in a sub-zero dawn to find the furnace cold and the pipes frozen, or the exhilaration of changing a tire by flashlight in an icy garage. No wonder his muscles atrophy as he lies abed until noon, nibbling bits of toast over the latest edition. No wonder his horizons shrink and his waistband swells. And no wonder he'll live twice as long as I will.

When I pitched my silken pavilion in the Appalachian foothills and challenged Nature to knock the chip off my shoulder, I had a buoyant vision of the future. In it I was a bull-necked sport in a Tattersall vest ordering retrievers to heel and vilifying the Securities Exchange Commission. Peering deep into the crystal ball, I saw myself cantering across my freehold on a fat cob, cheered on by a devoted peasantry. To prepare for the role, I put in an intensive half hour each morning ingesting chutney, rustling the *New York Times*, and snarling apoplectically at the CIO. The results were unique but disappointing. In two weeks I had a superb duodenal ulcer and a wheeze like a noonday factory whistle. Although I doggedly mounted every cog I could find, the kernels merely shriveled up and I never moved an inch.

It was years before I realized my talents were

technical rather than executive and I slipped gracefully into the post of janitor and general scavenger of my farm. Humble as the duties are, they entail certain grave responsibilities. To me falls the task of grading and sorting the household refuse, of deciding what shall be retained and what discarded. One tiny slip, one moment's heedlessness, and a vital fruit rind or chop bone might find itself in the wrong category. Secondary to this work, though equally important, is the task of cataloguing wastepaper and bottles, which I prefer to shoulder myself rather than assign to subordinates. Wielding a stick tipped with a nail, I patrol the grounds like a park employee (though much worse paid), and spear any trash I deem offensive. Here again I exercise complete authority; if I see a piece of paper I feel like ignoring, I just don't spear it. What I mean is, the final decision rests with me.

This phase complete, I now turn my findings over to another bureau, of which I am head coordinator, for disposal. I place the containers in a special rickety wheelbarrow, and surrounding myself with a swarm of flies to render us invisible to enemy aircraft, proceed straight uphill to a pit about a quarter of a mile away. En route, I convoy my burden through two barbed-wire fences, an operation that produces several salty phrases frowned on by the postal authorities. I thereupon hurl the refuse into the pit with a single deft sprain of the back, set fire to the papers, and, filling my lungs with pungent, satisfying smoke, repair to my desk, too exhausted to move the rest of the day.

In winter, naturally, the pressure intensifies and I could almost use another pair of hands in addition to the two heads my enemies maintain I have. After lengthy consultation with a heating engineer now in Matteawan, my wife and I installed a pipeless furnace inlaid with emeralds and jade which feeds the warmth directly into an upstairs clothes closet, leaving the rest of the establishment at the freezing point. This ingenious arrangement has two advantages: it scents the house with an acrid, invigorating smell of frying cloth recalling a tailor shop in the Bronx, and it permits me to tend two kerosene burners, a Franklin stove, and a fireplace. The children have grown to accept the sooty-faced character with the icicle depending from his nose and the large drum of oil as some weird kind of minstrel, and it's probably just as well. What with two spectacular explosions to my credit and a reek like a gas-station attendant, I'm lucky they let me eat in the house. How anybody stays penned up in a sweltering hotel with cracked ice and a blonde is beyond me. I guess the human body can take an awful lot of punishment.